I am delighted that Keswick's 2018 focus   ɘ
world's clearest and most compelling mi:
treasure trove for us to take back to our 1   ;
go beyond the usual sound bites – giving   'r
of the Holy Spirit in mission, the joy the ı _____ ...ge .. .. world, and
the role for us all.

Anna Bishop, Executive Director, Global Connections: the UK Network for World Mission (www.globalconnections.org.uk)

I love the way this study guide so clearly teaches us the Bible to encourage us to reach out to the world. There is a profound conviction here that knowledge of the truth will lead to godliness (Titus 1:1). And, of course, to be godly is to be like God, who so loved the world that he sent his Son to die – a fact that is all the more staggering when we realize from the first study that 'the underlying reason for mission is God's desire that others share his pleasure in his Son'.

Rico Tice, Senior Minister for Evangelism, All Souls, Langham Place, London, and the co-author of Christianity Explored

Sent

Serving God's Mission

Tim Chester

BIBLE STUDY RESOURCES FOR
INDIVIDUALS OR SMALL GROUPS

INTER-VARSITY PRESS
36 Causton Street, London SW1P 4ST, England
Email: ivp@ivpbooks.com
Website: www.ivpbooks.com

First published 2018

British Library Cataloguing-in-Publication Data
A catalogue record for this book is available from the British Library.

ISBN: 978–1–78359–654–6
eBook ISBN: 978–1–78359–655–3

Set in Warnock
Typeset in Great Britain by CRB Associates, Potterhanworth, Lincolnshire
Printed in Great Britain by Ashford Colour Press Ltd, Gosport, Hampshire

Contents

Introduction

It's all too easy not to think much about mission. Every now and then we might write a cheque or attend a prayer meeting. But we can often think of mission as something that is done some*where* else by some*one* else.

But mission is not done somewhere else. Jesus says, 'You will be my witnesses in Jerusalem, and in all Judea and Samaria, and to the ends of the earth' (Acts 1:8). Yes, mission is about reaching unreached people around the globe. But it's also about reaching neighbours and friends in our town (our 'Jerusalem') and our region (our 'Judea and Samaria'). Mission begins on your doorstep and reaches across the world.

And mission is not done by someone else. Jesus gave the task of mission to us, to you. He didn't say, 'They shall be my witnesses' or 'People in mission agencies shall be my witnesses.' He said, 'You shall be my witnesses.' Not all of us will go to other cultures. But all of us should be involved in sending, praying, giving. The great nineteenth-century preacher Charles H. Spurgeon said, 'Every Christian is either a missionary or an imposter.'

Reaching unreached people for Christ is our job. It's your job. And this study guide explores the 'job description' provided by the Bible.

This study guide can be used as a companion to *Mission Matters: Love Says Go* by Tim Chester (IVP, 2016). *Mission Matters* is part of the Keswick Foundations series. You don't need access to *Mission Matters* to use this study guide. But each study suggests a chapter or chapters from *Mission Matters* that will extend or deepen your understanding of the subject.

SESSION 1

The Father's love

▶ GETTING STARTED

For over 1,500 years the church used the word 'mission' to describe what God does rather than what we do. It comes from a Latin word, which means 'send'. We use it today to talk about sending people out, into our neighbourhoods or across the globe. But we are sent because first of all:

- God the Father sent his Son into the world to rescue his people;
- God the Father sends his Spirit to empower us to be his witnesses.

Mission doesn't start with us. It starts with God.

READ *John 17:20-26*

²⁰*My prayer is not for them alone. I pray also for those who will believe in me through their message,* ²¹*that all of them may be one, Father, just as you are in me and I am in you. May they also be in us so that the world may believe that you have sent me.* ²²*I have given them the glory that you gave me, that they may be one as we are one –* ²³*I in them and you in me – so that they may be brought to complete unity. Then the world will know that you sent me and have loved them even as you have loved me.*

²⁴*Father, I want those you have given me to be with me where I am, and to see my glory, the glory you have given me because you loved me before the creation of the world.*

²⁵*Righteous Father, though the world does not know you, I know you, and they know that you have sent me.* ²⁶*I have made you known to them, and will continue to make you known in order that the love you have for me may be in them and that I myself may be in them.*

FOCUS ON THE THEME

1. Identify reasons for getting involved in world mission.

WHAT DOES THE BIBLE SAY?

2. According to John 17:20–26, who is sent and what is he sent to do?

3.   According to verse 24, what is the reason for mission?

4.   Identify the ways in which Jesus shares his experience of the Father with us.

The chief end of missions is not the salvation of men but the glory of God.

(Samuel Zwemer, *Thinking Missions with Christ*, p. 67)

◎ GOING DEEPER

5.   Read Revelation 7:9–17. What do we learn about the scope of mission from this passage?

6.   What are people doing in this passage? How does this connect to the reason for mission in John 17?

7.   What reasons does this passage give us for worshipping Jesus?

Lack of interest in mission is not fundamentally caused by an absence of compassion or commitment . . . Shocking statistics, gruesome stories or emotionally manipulative commands to obedience only go so far . . . Lack of interest in mission is best remedied by intensifying people's passion for Christ, so that the passions of his heart become the passions that propel our hearts.

(Tim A. Dearborn, *Beyond Duty*, pp. 16–17, 30)

 **LIVING IT OUT**

8. In John 17:18 Jesus prays, 'As you sent me into the world, I have sent them into the world.' How is our mission like the mission of Jesus?

9. How might the Father's delight in the Son reshape our attitude to mission?

10. In verse 23, Jesus prays for the unity of the church so that people will believe in him. How does the life of your church display the love of God in Christ?

 **PRAYER TIME**

'[I pray] that they may be brought to complete unity. Then the world will know that you sent me and have loved them even as you have loved me' (verse 23). Use the prayer of Jesus to shape your prayers for your church and the churches in your region.

 **FURTHER STUDY**

Read chapter 1 of *Mission Matters*.

SESSION 2

The Son's name

▶ GETTING STARTED

A man knocks at your door in the middle of the night. What do you do?

Suppose you hear him shout, 'My name's John Smith. Please let me in.' What's your response? You'll probably shout back, 'Who are you and why should I let you in?'

But suppose he shouts, 'Open up in the name of the law.' Through the glass of the door you see a policeman's uniform. In this case you'll let him in as quickly as possible. (Unless, of course, you're a criminal, in which case you're already heading out the back!)

The Christian gospel is a declaration of good news that comes with a command. It is the good news that Jesus has died in our place and risen to give us eternal life. And it comes with the command to believe and repent. Jesus told us to go to all nations, 'teaching them to obey everything I have commanded you' (Matthew 28:20).

But if we're going to call people to faith and repentance, and if people are going to listen, then we need to know by what authority we speak.

READ *Acts 4:1-22*

¹ *The priests and the captain of the temple guard and the Sadducees came up to Peter and John while they were speaking to the people.* ² *They were greatly disturbed because the apostles were teaching the people, proclaiming in Jesus the resurrection of the dead.* ³ *They seized Peter and John and, because it was evening, they put them in jail until the next day.* ⁴ *But many who heard the message believed; so the number of men who believed grew to about five thousand.*

⁵ *The next day the rulers, the elders and the teachers of the law met in Jerusalem.* ⁶ *Annas the high priest was there, and so were Caiaphas, John, Alexander and others of the high priest's family.* ⁷ *They had Peter and John brought before them and began to question them: 'By what power or what name did you do this?'*

⁸ *Then Peter, filled with the Holy Spirit, said to them: 'Rulers and elders of the people!* ⁹ *If we are being called to account today for an act of kindness shown to a man who was lame and are being asked how he was healed,* ¹⁰ *then know this, you and all the people of Israel: it is by the name of Jesus Christ of Nazareth, whom you crucified but whom God raised from the dead, that this man stands before you healed.* ¹¹ *Jesus is*

> *"the stone you builders rejected,*
>   *which has become the cornerstone."*

¹² *Salvation is found in no one else, for there is no other name under heaven given to mankind by which we must be saved.'*

¹³ *When they saw the courage of Peter and John and realised that they were unschooled, ordinary men, they were astonished and they took note that these men had been with Jesus.* ¹⁴ *But since they could see the man who had been healed standing there with them, there was nothing they could say.* ¹⁵ *So they ordered them to withdraw from the Sanhedrin and then conferred together.* ¹⁶ *'What are we going to do with these men?' they asked. 'Everyone living in Jerusalem knows they have performed a notable sign, and we cannot deny it.* ¹⁷ *But to stop this thing from*

spreading any further among the people, we must warn them to speak no longer to anyone in this name.'

[18] *Then they called them in again and commanded them not to speak or teach at all in the name of Jesus.* [19] *But Peter and John replied, 'Which is right in God's eyes: to listen to you, or to him? You be the judges!* [20] *As for us, we cannot help speaking about what we have seen and heard.'*

[21] *After further threats they let them go. They could not decide how to punish them, because all the people were praising God for what had happened.* [22] *For the man who was miraculously healed was over forty years old.*

FOCUS ON THE THEME

1. When are you happy being told what to do? When are you *not* happy being told what to do?

WHAT DOES THE BIBLE SAY?

2. In verse 7 the religious leaders ask, 'By what power or what name did you do this?' Summarize Peter's answer.

3. Look at verses 10–12. Why is there authority in the name of Jesus?

4. Look at Acts 3:1–10. What is the impact of the name of Jesus on the lame man?

If God desires every knee to bow to Jesus and every tongue to confess him, so should we. We should be 'jealous' for the honour of his name – troubled when it remains unknown, hurt when it is ignored, indignant when it is blasphemed, and all the time anxious and determined that it shall be given the honour and glory which are due to it. The highest of all missionary motives is neither obedience to the Great Commission (important as that is), nor love for sinners who are alienated and perishing (strong as that incentive is, especially when we contemplate the wrath of God), but rather zeal – burning and passionate zeal – for the glory of Jesus Christ.

(John Stott, *The Message of Romans*, p. 53)

◎ GOING DEEPER

5. According to Romans 10:9–13, how are people saved from God's judgment?

6. According to Romans 10:9–13, *who* are saved from God's judgment?

7. Trace the links in the chain of Paul's argument in Romans 10:13–17. What are the implications for us?

♥ LIVING IT OUT

8. How does Peter's response in Acts 4:12 help us counter those who claim it is arrogant for Christians to impose their views on other people or other cultures?

9. Look at Acts 3:6. How should this story guide our response when we feel unable to help people?

10. Look at Acts 4:19–20. How should this story shape our response when we're told it's inappropriate to speak about Jesus?

What we are claiming is nothing to do with ourselves. It is not about how wonderful Christians are, how great a religion we have, and the answers we have come up with for the world's problems. No, it is not a claim about ourselves, it is simply a witness and a testimony to what the Scriptures –

*the Old and New Testament – tell us about the one true living God, and
how and where and through whom this living God has acted in order to
bring salvation to us and to the whole of creation.*

(Christopher Wright at the Keswick Convention)

 PRAYER TIME

Pray for the persecuted church. Pray for two or three specific Christians
who are in prison for proclaiming Christ. There are a number of
organizations that can provide up-to-date information to help you pray
for the persecuted church.

 FURTHER STUDY

Read chapters 2 and 7 of *Mission Matters*.

SESSION 3

The Spirit's power

▶ GETTING STARTED

'Batteries not included'. There's nothing more frustrating for a young child than receiving a longed-for Christmas present only to find that batteries are not included. The present offers so much promise, but that promise is unrealized. The remote-controlled car or speaking doll sits on the floor, amidst the discarded wrapping paper, as if mocking the child's frustrated hopes.

'You will be my witnesses in Jerusalem, and in all Judea and Samaria, and to the ends of the earth.' That's what Jesus said at the beginning of Acts, just before he ascended into heaven (Acts 1:8). What an amazing promise!

But are the batteries included? Does Jesus empower us for the task he gives us? Yes, he does. His call to be his witnesses is preceded by these words: 'You will receive power when the Holy Spirit comes on you; and you will be my witnesses ...' That promise was fulfilled on the day of Pentecost in Acts 2. And in Acts 4 we see what that promise looks like in practice.

READ *Acts 4:23-31*

²³ *On their release, Peter and John went back to their own people and reported all that the chief priests and the elders had said to them.* ²⁴ *When they heard this, they raised their voices together in prayer to God. 'Sovereign Lord,' they said, 'you made the heavens and the earth and the sea, and everything in them.* ²⁵ *You spoke by the Holy Spirit through the mouth of your servant, our father David:*

> *"'Why do the nations rage*
> *and the peoples plot in vain?*
> ²⁶ *The kings of the earth rise up*
> *and the rulers band together*
> *against the Lord*
> *and against his anointed one."*

²⁷ *Indeed Herod and Pontius Pilate met together with the Gentiles and the people of Israel in this city to conspire against your holy servant Jesus, whom you anointed.* ²⁸ *They did what your power and will had decided beforehand should happen.* ²⁹ *Now, Lord, consider their threats and enable your servants to speak your word with great boldness.* ³⁰ *Stretch out your hand to heal and perform signs and wonders through the name of your holy servant Jesus.'*

³¹ *After they prayed, the place where they were meeting was shaken. And they were all filled with the Holy Spirit and spoke the word of God boldly.*

 FOCUS ON THE THEME

1. What makes mission daunting – whether that involves going to your neighbourhood or around the globe?

WHAT DOES THE BIBLE SAY?

2. What is making mission daunting for the Christians in Acts 4?

3. How does the wording of their prayer reflect the challenge they faced?

4. What is the outcome of their prayer?

GOING DEEPER

5. Look at Acts 4:8 and 13. What has been the Spirit's impact already in this story?

6. Look at Acts 6:10; 7:55; 8:26–31; 10:19–20, 44–46; 13:1–3 and 16:6–7. How do we see the Spirit at work in the growth of the church?

7. In the light of the Spirit's work in the book of Acts, what would we expect a Spirit-filled church to be like?

Supposing we had awakened today to find everything concerning the Holy Spirit and prayer removed from the Bible ... What difference would it make practically between the way we worked yesterday and the way we would work today, and tomorrow? What difference would it make in the majority of Christians' practical work and plans? ... Isn't much work done by human talent, energy, and clever ideas? Where does the supernatural power of God have a real place?

(Francis Schaeffer, cited in *L'Abri*, pp. 64–65)

 LIVING IT OUT

8. Imagine Jesus had not sent the Spirit to empower us to be his witnesses. How would we approach the task of mission without the Spirit?

9. What difference does – or should – the gift of the Spirit make to the way we approach the task of mission?

10. What should we do when we find mission daunting?

When Henry Martyn, that splendid young hero of the cross, lay dying with a fever in Persia, he received a letter asking how the missionary interest of the church at home could be increased. The dying saint said, 'Tell them to live more with Christ, to catch more of His Spirit, for the spirit of Christ is the spirit of missions, and the nearer we get to Him, the more intensely missionary we become.'

(Cited by Lettie Cowman, *Charles E. Cowman: Missionary Warrior*, p. 116)

▲ PRAYER TIME

Use the prayer of verses 24–30 to shape your prayers:

- Praise God for his sovereign, creative power (verse 24).
- Confess your part in humanity's continual opposition to God that came to a climax at the cross (verses 25–27).
- Thank God for using the death of Christ to bring salvation to the world and using the persecution of the church to spread that message (verse 28).
- Ask God for boldness to speak his word (verses 29–30).

● FURTHER STUDY

Read chapter 3 of *Mission Matters*.

SESSION 4

The Bible's story

▶ GETTING STARTED

Who in your church is interested in world mission? Perhaps you can list some names. Maybe you have a mission committee who keep banging the drum for world mission. Maybe it's a few individuals who have made it 'their thing'.

There's perhaps a sense of 'out of sight, out of mind'. We see local needs every day with our own eyes. But we don't see the needs of the lost in other countries unless we choose to look. And so it's all too easy for world mission to be a peripheral activity in the life of a local church.

But world mission is not a peripheral activity in the story of the Bible. We may not always see the needs of the lost around the world, but we can see the centrality of mission in our Bibles. The Bible itself is always putting mission back at the top of the agenda.

READ *Luke 24:36–49*

³⁶ *While they were still talking about this, Jesus himself stood among them and said to them, 'Peace be with you.'*

³⁷ *They were startled and frightened, thinking they saw a ghost.* ³⁸ *He said to them, 'Why are you troubled, and why do doubts rise in your minds?* ³⁹ *Look at my hands and my feet. It is I myself! Touch me and see; a ghost does not have flesh and bones, as you see I have.'*

⁴⁰ *When he had said this, he showed them his hands and feet.* ⁴¹ *And while they still did not believe it because of joy and amazement, he asked them, 'Do you have anything here to eat?'* ⁴² *They gave him a piece of broiled fish,* ⁴³ *and he took it and ate it in their presence.*

⁴⁴ *He said to them, 'This is what I told you while I was still with you: everything must be fulfilled that is written about me in the Law of Moses, the Prophets and the Psalms.'*

⁴⁵ *Then he opened their minds so they could understand the Scriptures.* ⁴⁶ *He told them, 'This is what is written: the Messiah will suffer and rise from the dead on the third day,* ⁴⁷ *and repentance for the forgiveness of sins will be preached in his name to all nations, beginning at Jerusalem.* ⁴⁸ *You are witnesses of these things.* ⁴⁹ *I am going to send you what my Father has promised; but stay in the city until you have been clothed with power from on high.'*

FOCUS ON THE THEME

1. What Bible passage would you use if you had to give a talk on world mission?

◉ WHAT DOES THE BIBLE SAY?

2. This is the first time most of the disciples have met the risen Christ on the first Easter day. What does Jesus do?

3. What's the content of Jesus' teaching?

4. Where in the Bible does Jesus go to find this teaching?

The whole Bible is itself a missional phenomenon. The writings that now comprise our Bible are themselves the product of and witness to the ultimate mission of God. The Bible renders to us the story of God's mission through God's people in their engagement with God's world for the sake of the whole of God's creation. The Bible is the drama of this God of purpose engaged in the mission of achieving that purpose universally, embracing past, present and future, Israel and the nations, 'life, the universe and everything,' and with its centre, focus, climax, and completion in Jesus Christ. Mission is not just one of a list of things that the Bible happens to talk about, only a bit more urgently than some. Mission is, in that much-abused phrase, 'what it's all about.'

(Christopher Wright, *The Mission of God*, p. 22)

◎ GOING DEEPER

5.   What does Paul say about mission to the nations in Galatians 3:7–9?

6.   According to Galatians 3:13–14, why was Christ cursed on the cross?

7.   According to Galatians 3:26–29, who are the true people of God?

♥ LIVING IT OUT

8.   Can you identify some of the ways we see mission to the nations in the Old Testament?

9.   How should the centrality of mission in the Bible story affect the way we view the Bible?

10. How should the centrality of mission in the Bible story affect the way we view mission?

There are the five parts of the Bible. The God of the Old Testament is a missionary God, calling one family in order to bless all the families of the earth. The Christ of the Gospels is a missionary Christ; he sent the church out to witness. The Spirit of the Acts is a missionary Spirit; he drove the church out from Jerusalem to Rome. The church of the epistles is a missionary church, a worldwide community with a worldwide vocation. The end of the Revelation is a missionary End, a countless throng from every nation. So I think we have to say the religion of the Bible is a missionary religion. The evidence is overwhelming and irrefutable. Mission cannot be regarded as a regrettable lapse from tolerance or decency. Mission cannot be regarded as the hobby of a few fanatical eccentrics in the church. Mission lies at the heart of God and therefore at the very heart of the church. A church without mission is no longer a church. It is contradicting an essential part of its identity. The church is mission.

(John Stott, *Authentic Christianity*, pp. 315–316)

▲ PRAYER TIME

After this I looked, and there before me was a great multitude that no one could count, from every nation, tribe, people and language, standing before the throne and before the Lamb. They were wearing white robes and were holding palm branches in their hands. And they cried out in a loud voice:

> *'Salvation belongs to our God,*
> *who sits on the throne,*
> *and to the Lamb.'*

(Revelation 7:9–10)

Find out about one unreached people group. Use that information to pray for mission to those people so that, one day, individuals from that people group will be part of the great multitude who praise Jesus the Lamb.

 **FURTHER STUDY**

Read chapters 4 and 5 of *Mission Matters*.

The church's task

▶ GETTING STARTED

Do you think you could be a missionary? What would it take? What training would you need? Where would you go?

Peter tells us that we're all missionaries. Being a missionary is not something you achieve. It's an identity you're given in Christ. And mission is not necessarily something you go to do somewhere else in the world. Your home, workplace and neighbourhood are a mission field.

Mission is here. Mission is now. Mission is you.

READ *1 Peter 2:9–12*

> [9]*But you are a chosen people, a royal priesthood, a holy nation, God's special possession, that you may declare the praises of him who called you out of darkness into his wonderful light.* [10]*Once you were not a people, but now you are the people of God; once you had not received mercy, but now you have received mercy.*
>
> [11]*Dear friends, I urge you, as foreigners and exiles, to abstain from sinful desires, which wage war against your soul.* [12]*Live such good lives among the pagans that, though they accuse you of doing wrong, they may see your good deeds and glorify God on the day he visits us.*

 FOCUS ON THE THEME

1. Have you ever been chosen to do a particular job? How did you feel about that task?

 WHAT DOES THE BIBLE SAY?

2. How does Peter describe the *identity* of the church in these verses?

3. How does Peter describe the *task* of the church in these verses?

4. How should we expect the world to respond to the church as it lives out its new identity in Christ?

The church exists by mission as a fire exists by burning.

(Emil Brunner, *The Word and the World*, p. 108)

⊙ GOING DEEPER

5. According to 1 Peter 2:13–25, what happens when we live as holy citizens and workers?

6. According to 1 Peter 3:1–6, what might happen when we live as holy members of our families?

7. According to 1 Peter 2 – 3, how and where does mission take place?

♥ LIVING IT OUT

8. Mission includes our neighbourhood ('Jerusalem'), our region ('Judea and Samaria') and our world ('the ends of the earth') (Acts 1:8). In what ways are you a witness in your neighbourhood, workplace and home?

9. In what ways is your church a witness in your city or region?

10. In what ways is your church involved in mission around the world?

▲ PRAYER TIME

Pray for the mission involvement of your church and the missionaries you support:

- in your neighbourhood ('Jerusalem')
- in your region ('Judea and Samaria')
- in the world ('the ends of the earth')

● FURTHER STUDY

Read chapter 6 of *Mission Matters*.

SESSION 6

The cultural challenge

▶ GETTING STARTED

Imagine playing a familiar game with a new group of people. It gradually becomes apparent that they're playing by a different set of rules. They think you're a bit of an idiot and you feel as if they're ganging up on you. You've always been good at this game, but now you're incompetent.

This is how it feels living and working in a new culture. Each culture has its own set of rules and ways of thinking. These rules don't just cover what the culture considers polite behaviour – that's just the surface layer. It goes much deeper, to the way people see the world and their place in it.

But learning the new set of rules isn't easy. The problem is that most of the time local people can't tell you what the rules are. For them the rules are intuitive. But they *do* know when you break the rules!

No wonder missionaries usually feel incompetent when they first live in a new culture.

But missionaries are not just wrestling with the new culture. Encountering a different culture starts to raise questions about your home culture. Is this belief or that behaviour part of biblical teaching as I've always assumed, or is it actually just part of my culture? And how should I adapt to the local culture?

READ *1 Corinthians 9:19–27*

¹⁹ Though I am free and belong to no one, I have made myself a slave to everyone, to win as many as possible. ²⁰ To the Jews I became like a Jew, to win the Jews. To those under the law I became like one under the law (though I myself am not under the law), so as to win those under the law. ²¹ To those not having the law I became like one not having the law (though I am not free from God's law but am under Christ's law), so as to win those not having the law. ²² To the weak I became weak, to win the weak. I have become all things to all people so that by all possible means I might save some. ²³ I do all this for the sake of the gospel, that I may share in its blessings.

²⁴ Do you not know that in a race all the runners run, but only one gets the prize? Run in such a way as to get the prize. ²⁵ Everyone who competes in the games goes into strict training. They do it to get a crown that will not last; but we do it to get a crown that will last for ever. ²⁶ Therefore I do not run like someone running aimlessly; I do not fight like a boxer beating the air. ²⁷ No, I strike a blow to my body and make it my slave so that after I have preached to others, I myself will not be disqualified for the prize.

FOCUS ON THE THEME

1. Have you ever been in a social situation where you felt out of place? How did you feel?

◯ WHAT DOES THE BIBLE SAY?

2. What does Paul do when he encounters people from different cultures?

3. Why does Paul act in this way?

4. What is the cost to Paul of this adaptation?

Culture must always be tested and judged by Scripture. Because men and women are God's creatures, some of their culture is rich in beauty and goodness. Because they are fallen, all of it is tainted with sin and some of it is demonic. The gospel does not presuppose the superiority of any culture to another, but evaluates all cultures according to its own criteria of truth and righteousness, and insists on moral absolutes in every culture. Missions have all too frequently exported with the gospel an alien culture and churches have sometimes been in bondage to culture rather than to Scripture. Christ's evangelists must humbly seek to empty themselves of all but their personal authenticity in order to become the servants of others, and churches must seek to transform and enrich culture, all for the glory of God.

(The Lausanne Covenant)

◎ GOING DEEPER

5. Read Acts 10:1–23. What are the cultural taboos Peter has to overcome if the gospel is going to go to the Gentiles?

6. Read Acts 10:24–48. What are the results of Peter setting aside his cultural taboos?

7. Read Acts 11:1–3. How do people at home react to Peter's cross-cultural mission?

We all need to discern more clearly between Scripture and culture. For Scripture is the eternal, unchanging Word of God. But culture is an amalgam of ecclesiastical tradition and social convention. Whatever 'authority' culture may have is derived only from church and community. It cannot claim an immunity to criticism or reform. On the contrary, 'culture' changes from age to age and from place to place. Moreover, Christians, who say they desire to live under the authority of God's Word, should subject their own contemporary culture to continuing biblical scrutiny. Far from resenting or resisting cultural change, we should be in the forefront of those who propose and work for it provided of course that our critique of culture is made from a sound biblical perspective.

(John Stott, *Balanced Christianity*, pp. 30–31)

♥ LIVING IT OUT

8. How did people adapt to reach you?

9. How is your church adapting to reach different groups in its neighbourhood?

10. Living and working in a different culture can be confusing, unsettling and tiring, especially at first. How can you support your missionaries well?

▲ PRAYER TIME

Pray for the missionaries you support. Pray that they find their identity in Christ and not in their competence. Pray that God would help them understand the culture they're reaching. Pray that God would help them love the local people, especially when they're frustrated by the cultural differences.

● FURTHER STUDY

Read chapters 9 and 10 of *Mission Matters*.

The global mandate

▶ GETTING STARTED

What's your ambition? Pass your exams? Get married? Get promoted? Pay off the mortgage? Run a marathon? Swim with dolphins?

Paul has an ambition and he wants us to share it. That's why he writes to the church in Rome. He wants them to help him achieve his ambition.

And Paul's ambition is not just his own quirky obsession. The point of the letter to the Romans is that Paul's ambition arises out of the Bible story. This is God's ambition. And so this should be our ambition.

We'd better find out what it is . . .

READ *Romans 15:8–24*

⁸*For I tell you that Christ has become a servant of the Jews on behalf of God's truth, so that the promises made to the patriarchs might be confirmed* ⁹ *and, moreover, that the Gentiles might glorify God for his mercy. As it is written:*

> *'Therefore I will praise you among the Gentiles;*
>> *I will sing the praises of your name.'*

¹⁰*Again, it says,*

> *'Rejoice, you Gentiles, with his people.'*

¹¹*And again,*

> *'Praise the Lord, all you Gentiles;*
>> *let all the peoples extol him.'*

¹²*And again, Isaiah says,*

> *'The Root of Jesse will spring up,*
>> *one who will arise to rule over the nations;*
>> *in him the Gentiles will hope.'*

¹³*May the God of hope fill you with all joy and peace as you trust in him, so that you may overflow with hope by the power of the Holy Spirit.*

¹⁴*I myself am convinced, my brothers and sisters, that you yourselves are full of goodness, filled with knowledge and competent to instruct one another.* ¹⁵*Yet I have written to you quite boldly on some points to remind you of them again, because of the grace God gave me* ¹⁶*to be a minister of Christ Jesus to the Gentiles. He gave me the priestly duty of proclaiming the gospel of God, so that the Gentiles might become an offering acceptable to God, sanctified by the Holy Spirit.*

¹⁷*Therefore I glory in Christ Jesus in my service to God.* ¹⁸*I will not venture to speak of anything except what Christ has accomplished through me in leading the Gentiles to obey God by what I have said and done –* ¹⁹*by the power of signs and wonders, through the power of the Spirit of God. So from Jerusalem all the way round to Illyricum, I have*

fully proclaimed the gospel of Christ. [20]*It has always been my ambition to preach the gospel where Christ was not known, so that I would not be building on someone else's foundation.* [21]*Rather, as it is written:*

> *'Those who were not told about him will see,*
> *and those who have not heard will understand.'*

[22]*This is why I have often been hindered from coming to you.*

[23]*But now that there is no more place for me to work in these regions, and since I have been longing for many years to visit you,* [24]*I plan to do so when I go to Spain. I hope to see you while passing through and that you will assist me on my journey there, after I have enjoyed your company for a while.*

FOCUS ON THE THEME

1. What's on your 'bucket list' – the things you hope to do before you die?

WHAT DOES THE BIBLE SAY?

2. What point is Paul making in verses 8–12?

3. How does Paul view his ministry to the nations, according to verses 15–19?

4. How does Paul describe his ambition? And what has Paul's ambition got to do with the church in Rome?

It is the whole business of the whole church to preach the whole gospel to the whole world.

(Charles H. Spurgeon)

⊙ GOING DEEPER

5. Compare the beginning and end of Romans. What similarities can you spot between 1:1–7 and 16:25–27?

6. What does Paul say about the Gentiles or nations in these verses?

7. What do this introduction and conclusion suggest are the central themes of Paul's life?

 LIVING IT OUT

8. Reaching unreached people with the gospel is not someone else's
    job – it's our job. What might it mean for you to take ownership
    of the task of reaching unreached people?

9. As you look back on our studies, what have you learnt or seen
    in a fresh way?

10. What are you going to start doing as an individual? As a group
    or church?

Go, send, or disobey.

(John Piper)

PRAYER TIME

Identify three new actions you want to take in order to play your role in
reaching the world for Christ. Pray that God will help you fulfil these well
and use your contributions in his global purposes.

FURTHER STUDY

Read chapters 8 and 11 of *Mission Matters*.

Notes for leaders

As stated in the introduction, this study guide can be used as a companion to *Mission Matters: Love Says Go* by Tim Chester (IVP, 2016). You don't need to read *Mission Matters* to lead these studies. But you will find it useful background reading. Each session ends by identifying the chapter or chapters from *Mission Matters* relevant to that study.

The Father's love

Summary: This session is an encouragement to recognize that mission begins with the Father's love for his Son and his desire to share that joy with others.

1. People might mention things such as the command of Christ (in the Great Commission of Matthew 28:18–20), the plight of the lost, the joy of service, the needs of the poor and the opportunities of the harvest (Matthew 9:37–38). These are all good answers.

2. Verses 21, 23 and 25 all say that Jesus is sent by God the Father. Verse 22 says Jesus was sent so that *we* might *share* his glory, and verse 24 says Jesus was sent so that *we* might *see* his glory. Verse 26 says Jesus was sent to make God known so that we might share the love of the Triune God.

3. Reason #1: 'I want those you have given me to be with me where I am.' God has given people to Christ to be in relationship with Christ as his bride (John 6:37; 17:2). So one reason for mission is to gather Christ's people into the church. But why? Reason #2: 'To see my glory, the glory you have given me.' The reason for mission is so that people will appreciate the glory of Christ. But why? Reason #3: 'Because you loved me before the creation of the world.' Throughout all eternity the Father has loved the Son. The underlying reason for mission is God's desire that others share his pleasure in his Son.

4. We are in the Father just as the Son is in the Father (verse 21). We receive glory just as the Son receives glory from the Father (verse 22). We know the Father just as the Son knows the Father (verses 25–26). We are loved by the Father just as Jesus is loved by the Father (verse 26).

5. Mission involves the gathering of 'a great multitude' who come 'from every nation, tribe, people and language' (verse 9). The scope of mission is global.

6. The great multitude are worshipping 'the Lamb', that is, Jesus. This is the fulfilment of God the Father's desire to see others sharing his pleasure in his Son. Jesus is at the centre of everything (verse 17).

7. Jesus is the Lamb who brings salvation (verse 10). Alongside God the Father, he is worthy of praise, glory, wisdom, thanks, honour, power and strength (verse 12). He shelters his people in the midst of their suffering (verse 15). He is the shepherd who leads his people to living water, and through him God wipes away every tear (verse 17). The reason for mission is God's intent that others should worship his Son. This happens not because God forces people to worship Jesus, but because Jesus is so revealed in history that his people have endless reasons to worship him.

8. There are many ways in which this question could be answered. People may talk about how *what* we do or the *way* we do it is like the mission of Jesus. But make sure people also note the *goal* of mission: like Jesus, we are sent so that others might share the joy and love of the Trinity. (There are some important differences between what Jesus did and what we do. Jesus is the Saviour of the world, while we only point to the Saviour.)

9. We can think our job is to persuade people to do something they will find unpleasant. And our message is a call to self-denial and sacrifice. But at a more fundamental level, we are calling people to share the infinite joy and love of the Triune God.

10. Jesus is talking here not about institutional unity, but about the everyday relationships of Christians – this is what is seen by the world. According to 1 Peter 3:8–15, we are called to 'be like-minded, be sympathetic, love one another, be compassionate and humble', so that we provoke questions about our hope. Your church displays the love of God in Christ as you care for one another, as you forgive one another, and as you are committed to one another despite your racial and social differences.

SESSION 2

The Son's name

Summary: This session is an encouragement to recognize the implications of Christ being the only hope of the world.

1. There are no right or wrong answers to this question. But the chances are that people will be happy to be told what to do when either (1) someone has authority over them, or (2) they need help. Both answers are relevant to our theme. We should be happy to be told what to do by Jesus (or his representatives) because (1) he has authority over us and (2) we are in desperate need of his help ('salvation is found in no one else', as verse 12 says). Don't make these connections before you have explored the text together, but you may want to draw them out at appropriate points as your Bible study unfolds.

2. After pointing out that their 'crime' is an act of kindness (verse 9), Peter says they are acting in the name of Jesus. In other words, their 'power' or authority comes from Jesus.

3. To Peter's hearers, the name of Jesus carried no weight. They thought of Jesus as the criminal who had recently been executed by the Romans. But Peter says God has raised him from the dead (verse 10). Jesus had been rejected by humanity, but now he has been vindicated by God (verse 11). Moreover, Jesus is the only one who can save (verse 12).

4. The lame man is healed 'instantly' (3:7). He is also healed completely – he 'became strong' (3:7). He goes from lame to leaping and from begging to praising (3:8). The word 'healed' in 4:9 is literally 'saved'. What happened to the lame man is a visible and dramatic example of the saving power of Jesus.

5. Verses 9–10 say that we are saved by believing in our hearts and professing with our mouths that Jesus is the risen Lord. Verse 11 says we are saved by believing in him. Verses 12–13 say we are saved by calling on his name.

6. Verse 11 says '*anyone* who believes' is saved. In particular, Paul highlights the fact that Jews and Gentiles are saved in the same way (verse 12). In other words, Jesus is the only hope of salvation for people, irrespective of their religious, social, ethnic, economic or racial background. This is particularly relevant when people argue that we should not try to convert sincere adherents of other religions.

7. (1) Calling on the name of Jesus requires (2) believing in Jesus, which requires (3) hearing about Jesus, which requires (4) someone proclaiming Jesus, which requires (5) someone being sent to proclaim Jesus. Thankfully, someone has been sent by God to proclaim Jesus: you! This is why Paul quotes from Isaiah 52:7: 'How beautiful are the feet of those who bring good news!' Verse 17 summarizes this 'chain': faith requires hearing, and hearing requires proclamation of 'the word about Christ'.

8. Christians are not recruiting members for their 'club'. We are offering the only hope of salvation. Nor are Christians claiming to be superior, as if we alone are clever or moral enough to know God. We do not proclaim our merits or even the merits of Christianity as a religious system. We proclaim the merits of Christ. He, and he alone, is the Saviour.

9. Peter lacked the financial resources to help the lame man. But he could proclaim the name of Jesus. We can't always solve people's emotional or physical problems. Nor can we always heal those who are sick. But we can always point them to Jesus. For Jesus offers ultimate hope – the hope of life beyond death in a world without tears.

10. Peter responds in two ways to the command not to speak about Jesus. First, he says Christians must obey God rather than people. Second, he says Christians can't help speaking about Jesus. We need to apply these truths with wisdom and gentleness – we're not to force our message on people (1 Peter 3:16). But we must resist peer pressure and legal pressure to keep quiet about Jesus.

SESSION 3

The Spirit's power

Summary: This session is an encouragement to recognize that we are not left to our own resources.

1. There are no right or wrong answers to this question. Don't feel the need at this point to correct 'wrong' feelings. This is a chance for everyone to talk without having to worry about getting the answer wrong.

2. Verse 23 picks up the story we explored in the previous session. You may want to invite people to recap. Peter and John have been imprisoned and then told to stop speaking about Jesus, something they have refused to do. This is the first time in its history that the church has been persecuted. The full might of the Jewish establishment is ranged against this small band of largely uneducated Christians.

3. Faced with the threat of persecution, the response of the believers was to pray. They address God as 'Sovereign Lord' and praise his power in creation. Though they feel small compared to their persecutors, they pray to an all-powerful God. They quote from Psalm 2, which shows that their persecution is part of humanity's opposition to God throughout history. They link their persecution to Christ's cross – they are following in the footsteps of their Saviour. They recognize that, though the crucifixion and their persecution are evil acts, they are also part of God's plan. They don't pray for the persecution to go away. Instead, they pray for boldness to speak of Christ in the face of threats as God performs miraculous signs. That's because the last time God performed a miracle (chapter 3), their leaders were thrown into prison (chapter 4).

4. Verse 31 says, 'After they prayed, the place where they were meeting was shaken. And they were all filled with the Holy Spirit and spoke the

word of God boldly'. They needed boldness, they prayed for boldness and they received boldness. The shaking of the building recalls the day of Pentecost (Acts 2:2), which also led to proclamation.

5. Peter is an uneducated fisherman from a provincial backwater. Yet he speaks with courage before the Jewish establishment (verse 13). The reason is that he speaks 'filled with the Holy Spirit' (verse 8).

6. You could divide these passages between sub-groups. The Spirit enables God's people to confound opposition (6:10) and comforts them when they are persecuted (7:55). The Spirit creates opportunities to proclaim the gospel (8:26–31; 10:19–20) and enables those who hear to put their faith in Christ (10:44–46). The Spirit causes local churches to send out their best people in mission (13:1–3) and coordinates their missionary activity (16:6–7).

7. There are a number of possible answers to this question, but the key one for the purpose of this study is that a Spirit-filled church will have a concern for mission in its neighbourhood ('in Jerusalem'), in its region ('in all Judea and Samaria') and around the world ('to the ends of the earth') (Acts 1:8).

8. Without the Spirit, we would have to rely on our own abilities, strategies and energy. We would likely be fearful and hesitant.

9. Highlight the gap that exists between the answer to questions 8 and 9. Or highlight the gap that *should* exist, for it may be that people's response to question 8 describes their approach to mission now. If we are fearful, it may be because we're not praying for courage from the Spirit. If we lack opportunities, it may be because we're not prayerfully expecting the Spirit to send seeking people in our direction. If we're not experiencing the Spirit's help, it may be because we never put ourselves in a position where we need his help.

10. This is an opportunity to go back to question 1 and apply all that you have seen in Acts 4. The core answer will be that we should pray for boldness, and we can expect the Spirit to work in us and through us.

SESSION 4

The Bible's story

Summary: This session is an encouragement to recognize the centrality of mission to the Bible story.

1. There are lots of potential answers to this question. Most people are likely to suggest the Great Commission in Matthew 28:18–20. But push the group for other ideas. The aim is to begin to get people to think about how mission is a theme throughout the Bible and not just in one or two isolated places.

2. First, Jesus brings a word of peace (verses 36–38). Second, he invites them to touch his body and eats in their presence to prove that he is not a ghost, but has genuinely and bodily risen from the dead (verses 39–43). Third, he does a Bible study (verses 44–45). We might have expected the risen Christ on the first Easter day simply to declare truth. But instead, he turns to the Bible.

3. Jesus shows, first, that the Bible teaches that 'the Messiah will suffer and rise from the dead'. This is the gospel message – that we are saved through the death and resurrection of Jesus. Second, Jesus shows that the Bible teaches that forgiveness of sins will be preached to the nations. This is the gospel mission. The two big themes of the Bible are the gospel message and the gospel mission.

4. This teaching is found in 'the Law of Moses, the Prophets and the Psalms' (verse 44). The Jews divided the Bible into three sections:

   - the Torah or Law – what we call the Pentateuch;
   - the Prophets – including both the history books and prophetic books;
   - the Writings (often simply named 'the Psalms', as the book of Psalms was the largest book in the Writings) – what we call the wisdom books plus Ruth, Chronicles, Ezra, Nehemiah and Esther.

So 'the Law of Moses, the Prophets and the Psalms' includes the whole of the Old Testament.

To reinforce the point, you might want to ask, 'How does Jesus summarize the message of the Old Testament?' Answer: salvation through his death and resurrection, and mission to the nations. Mission to the nations is not a sub-plot to the Bible story; it's part of the central theme. It's not an occasional theme, but a key part of the Bible's message.

5. Paul says the inclusion of people from all nations was always part of God's plan. He describes the promise to Abraham as 'the gospel' announced in advance (verse 8).

6. The Jews were supposed to be a light to the nations, drawing the nations to God. Instead, they often profaned God's name. But now Jesus has redeemed 'us' (that is, believing Jews) through the cross so that the blessing of salvation might go to the Gentiles (the nations), just as God had promised Abraham. This is what happened after Jesus rose again. The first Christians were redeemed Jews, and they took the gospel to the nations. Today we continue that task.

7. People from every race (Jew and Gentile), social class (slave and free) and gender (male and female) can be part of God's people. What matters is faith in Christ. In other words, what matters is not who we are, but who Christ is. We are all one in Christ. So we take the gospel to all nations, all classes and both genders.

8. Abraham and his family were chosen to be a blessing to all nations (Genesis 12:3; 18:18–19). The law was given so Israel could embody God's goodness to the nations (Deuteronomy 4:5–8). The story of Ruth shows how the nations can find refuge as God's people live under God's rule. The expansion of the kingdom under David is a sign that all nations will submit to God's Messiah. Naaman illustrates how Gentiles can find salvation through faith in Israel's God (2 Kings 5). Jonah's life story is a prophetic call to Israel to proclaim God's grace to the nations. The servant of the Lord promised by Israel will embody the role of being a light to the Gentiles that Israel had largely failed to

fulfil (Isaiah 42:6; 49:6). Above all, the promised Saviour will bring salvation not only to Israel, but to the world.

9. As the beneficiaries of mission to the nations, it means we read the Bible (including the Old Testament) as *our* story. It also means we should expect to find the theme of mission throughout the Bible.

10. If mission to the nations is a central theme in the Bible, then it should be a central theme in our lives.

SESSION 5

The church's task

Summary: This session is an encouragement for people to recognize that mission is a task for everyone.

1. This is a chance for everyone to talk without having to worry about getting the answer wrong. Verse 9 says we have been chosen to model the character of God and declare his praises to the world.

2. Peter says the church is 'a chosen people', 'a royal priesthood', 'a holy nation', 'God's special possession', 'the people of God', recipients of mercy and 'foreigners and exiles' (verses 9–11). Most of these terms echo descriptions of God's people in the Old Testament (Isaiah 43:20; Exodus 19:5–6; Hosea 2:23). You might want to read Exodus 19:5–6 to explore what Peter has in mind when he describes the church in this way. God gave his people the law to show them how they could be a priestly nation (leading the nations to God as priests) and live in a way that reflected his character (being holy as he is holy). This is now the identity of the church.

3. Peter says we are to declare God's praises (verse 9) and live good lives that point people to God (verse 12). His description of our identity also carries implications for our behaviour. We are to be priestly, leading the nations to God (verse 9). We are to be holy like God and abstain from worldly ways (verse 11) so that we make God known to the world (verse 12).

4. Peter describes a twofold response. First, we can expect the world to be hostile. People will accuse us of doing wrong. Second, we can expect the world to be drawn to God. People will glorify God through our witness.

5. We are to respect everyone, honour our political leaders and submit to our masters. If we suffer for doing good (which probably means suffering because we follow Christ), then we are to remember that

Christ suffered for us. Verse 15 says that by doing good in this way we will 'silence the ignorant talk of foolish people'. You might invite the group to identify contemporary examples of 'the ignorant talk of foolish people' and then explore how our conduct might refute this.

6. Peter focuses on wives with unbelieving husbands. He calls them to witness to their husbands through their holy behaviour.

7. These verses do not say all there is to say about mission. But they do make it clear that mission is not just about preaching sermons at special events. Mission takes place as Christians live holy lives before a watching world. Mission takes place in our neighbourhoods, workplaces and homes. It is something in which we all play a part as God's royal priesthood and holy nation. We all live in a missionary location: our neighbourhoods, workplaces and homes!

8. This question begins by asking what people are already doing. It's important to affirm this. If people begin by talking about what they *should* be doing, encourage them to start with what they *are* doing. At some point, though, you might want to move on to think about whether there is anything new you could do, either individually or as a group.

9. This might include activities you do with other churches or plans to plant into nearby areas.

10. As with questions 8 and 9, this is an opportunity to affirm what you are already doing. But you may also want to extend the discussion to consider what else you could or should be doing.

The cultural challenge

Summary: This session is an encouragement to think about the challenges of communicating cross-culturally.

1. This is a chance for everyone to talk without having to worry about getting the answer wrong. It is also designed to begin to build some empathy with cross-cultural missionaries.

2. Paul adapts to new cultures. He tries to become like the people he wants to reach for Christ. But there are limits to Paul's adaptation to new cultures. He will not act contrary to Scripture (verse 21).

3. Paul wants 'to win as many as possible' (verses 19–21). He wants 'by all possible means' to 'save some' (verse 22). 'I do all this for the sake of the gospel' (verse 23). For Paul, this is a deliberate missionary strategy in which he sacrifices his own freedoms in Christ (verse 19) so he can win people for Christ.

4. Paul sacrifices his own freedoms (verse 19). In reaching the Jews, for example, he lives under aspects of the law of Moses that no longer apply to Christians (see Acts 21:17–26 for an example of this). Verses 24–27 are an indication that this adaptation is often hard work for Paul.

5. Acts 10 – 11 present a case study in cross-cultural mission. As a law-abiding Jew, Peter would not eat food that was unclean according to the law of Moses (10:14). That meant he would not eat with Gentiles for fear of contamination (10:28). For most of us, this may seem an example of a cultural practice that is obviously not part of the gospel. But for Peter, this was deeply engrained, not least because it was mandated by the law of Moses. Crossing cultures can be very unsettling!

6. Peter had the opportunity to proclaim the gospel to 'a large gathering' (10:27). As a result, 'the Holy Spirit came on all who heard the message' (10:44), and the gospel spread into new territory.

7. The Jewish believers in Judea were initially critical of Peter. This can also be the experience of cross-cultural missionaries. What do you think are the implications for those of us who send people to be cross-cultural missionaries?

8. This is an opportunity for people to see what the principles of 1 Corinthians 9 and Acts 10 look like in their own situation.

9. Begin by affirming the ways in which you are already adapting. Then you might want to consider what further adaptations you could make. You could also discuss how you can avoid adapting in ways that are contrary to Scripture. We're to lay aside our preferences in order to win people, but we can't win people to the gospel by laying aside the gospel! We may not want new converts to become like us, but we do want them to become like Jesus.

10. There are many answers to this question. A key is to appreciate the struggles they face. This means being patient with them and not having unrealistic expectations. It means encouraging them to find their identity in Christ and not in their competence. It means celebrating with them all the positives of the new culture. You might also brainstorm some practical ideas for encouraging missionaries, such as sending parcels of treats, making videos with greetings from home, calling them by Skype, emailing regular church news, giving them an eReader and sending them eBooks, and so on.

The global mandate

Summary: This session is an encouragement to own for ourselves the task of reaching the unreached.

1. There is no need at this stage to make people talk about mission. The aim is to set the scene and give everyone a chance to talk. On Paul's 'bucket list' is a trip to Spain (verse 24). But he's not hoping to go there because he wants to see the sights!

   As it happened, Paul never made it to Spain. His next stop was Jerusalem to deliver the collection he had made for Jewish Christians among Gentile churches (Romans 15:25–28). While he was in Jerusalem, he was arrested and taken to Rome (Acts 21:17, 27–33; 25:10–12; 28:16). There he is thought to have been martyred.

2. Christ came to save both Jews (verse 8) and Gentiles (verse 9). This is affirmed throughout the Old Testament, as illustrated by his quotes from 2 Samuel 22:50; Psalm 18:49; Deuteronomy 32:43; Psalm 117:1 and Isaiah 11:10. The word 'Gentiles' can also be translated 'nations' (since, for the Jews, all nations were Gentiles except themselves). Christ came for all nations.

3. Paul describes his mission to the nations as 'a priestly duty', with his converts as an offering of worship to God (verse 16). He also sees his ministry as a means by which Christ himself is leading the nations to God (verse 18). His accomplishments are really 'what Christ has accomplished through me' (verse 18). You could ask the follow-up question: 'How is involvement in world mission an act of worship?' Psalm 67 and Isaiah 12:4–5 should help you answer this question.

4. Paul's ambition is 'to preach the gospel where Christ was not known' (verse 20). Today we might say his ambition is to reach unreached people. The main reason why Paul is writing to the church in Rome is not to sort out some problem they have (verse 14). He is writing

to gain their support for his big ambition – his desire to take the gospel to new people and new places.

5. At both the beginning and end of Romans, Paul talks about:

    - the gospel;
    - which is made known in the prophetic writings (the Old Testament);
    - which is about Jesus;
    - and which is for all the Gentiles or nations;
    - to bring them to the obedience that comes from faith.

6. Paul was called by God to take the gospel to the nations (1:5). The nations are included in God's plan of salvation. They are called to 'the obedience that comes from faith' (1:5; 16:26) – that is, to turn to God in faith and repentance. The salvation of the nations is 'for his name's sake' (1:5; 16:27) – that is, it brings glory to Christ. The Roman Christians are themselves an example of this (1:6).

7. In Romans, Paul is concerned to show that the Bible is all about how the gospel of Jesus is for the nations. Much of the letter has explained how Paul's mission to the Gentiles is not his own innovation, but arises out of the Bible story. Romans is all about mission, and the Bible is all about mission. That's why Paul is all about mission!

8. Obviously you or your group can't reach the world on your own! But this is encouragement to see it as a task in which we can and should be involved. Mission agencies play a vital role in facilitating mission. But the local church can't leave the task to them. We all need to own the task by knowing, praying, giving, sending and perhaps going.

9–10. Questions 9 and 10 are an opportunity to ensure you put into practice what we have seen throughout these Bibles studies.

Books mentioned in the text

Introduction
Charles H. Spurgeon, 'A Sermon and a Reminiscence', *Sword and the Trowel* (March 1873), https://archive.spurgeon.org/s_and_t/srmn1873.php

Session 1: The Father's love
Samuel Zwemer, *Thinking Missions with Christ* (Marshall, Morgan & Scott, 1934)
Tim A. Dearborn, *Beyond Duty: A Passion for Christ, A Heart for Mission* (CreateSpace, 2nd edn, 2013)

Session 2: The Son's name
John Stott, *The Message of Romans*, The Bible Speaks Today series (IVP, 1994)
Christopher J. H. Wright, *Word to the World*, Keswick Year Book 2011 (Authentic, 2011)

Session 3: The Spirit's power
Francis Schaeffer, cited in Edith Schaeffer, *L'Abri* (Tyndale, 1969)
Lettie B. Cowman, *Charles E. Cowman: Missionary Warrior* (The Oriental Missionary Society, 1928)

Session 4: The Bible's story
Christopher J. H. Wright, *The Mission of God: Unlocking the Bible's Grand Narrative* (IVP, 2006)
John Stott, *Authentic Christianity: From the Writings of John Stott*, ed. Timothy Dudley-Smith (IVP, 1995)

Session 5: The church's task
Emil Brunner, *The Word and the World* (SCM Press, 1931)

Session 6: The cultural challenge

The Lausanne Covenant, www.lausanne.org/content/covenant/
lausanne-covenant

John Stott, *Balanced Christianity* (IVP, 2014)

Session 7: The global mandate

Charles H. Spurgeon, source unknown

John Piper, www.youtube.com/watch?v=W2UJQtdWb20

Other books on mission by the author

Good News to the Poor: Sharing the Gospel through Social Involvement
(IVP, 2004)

Total Church: A Radical Reshaping around Gospel and Community,
co-authored with Steve Timmis (IVP, 2007)

The Gospel-Centred Church, co-authored with Steve Timmis (The Good
Book Company, 2009)

*A Meal with Jesus: Discovering Grace, Community and Mission around
the Table* (IVP, 2011)

Everyday Church: Mission by Being Good Neighbours, co-authored with
Steve Timmis (IVP, 2011)

Unreached: Growing Churches in Working-Class and Deprived Areas
(IVP, 2012)

Crown of Thorns: Connecting Kingdom and Cross (Christian Focus, 2015)

Mission Matters: Love Says Go (IVP, 2015)

About Keswick Ministries

Our purpose

Keswick Ministries is committed to the spiritual renewal of God's people for his mission in the world.

God's purpose is to bring his blessing to all the nations of the world. That promise of blessing, which touches every aspect of human life, is ultimately fulfilled through the life, death, resurrection, ascension and future return of Christ. All of the people of God are called to participate in his missionary purposes, wherever he may place them. The central vision of Keswick Ministries is to see the people of God equipped, encouraged and refreshed to fulfil that calling, directed and guided by God's Word in the power of his Spirit, for the glory of his Son.

Our priorities

Keswick Ministries seeks to serve the local church through:

- **Hearing God's Word**: the Scriptures are the foundation for the church's life, growth and mission, and Keswick Ministries is committed to preach and teach God's Word in a way that is faithful to Scripture and relevant to Christians of all ages and backgrounds.

- **Becoming like God's Son**: from its earliest days the Keswick movement has encouraged Christians to live godly lives in the power of the Spirit, to grow in Christlikeness and to live under his lordship in every area of life. This is God's will for his people in every culture and generation.

- **Serving God's mission**: the authentic response to God's Word is obedience to his mission, and the inevitable result of Christlikeness is sacrificial service. Keswick Ministries seeks to encourage committed discipleship in family life, work and society, and energetic engagement in the cause of world mission.

Our ministry

- **Keswick: the event**. Every summer the town of Keswick hosts a three-week Convention, which attracts some 15,000 Christians from the UK and around the world. The event provides Bible teaching for all ages, vibrant worship, a sense of unity across generations and denominations, and an inspirational call to serve Christ in the world. It caters for children of all ages and has a strong youth and young adult programme. And it all takes place in the beautiful Lake District – a perfect setting for rest, recreation and refreshment.

- **Keswick: the movement**. For 140 years the work of Keswick has impacted churches worldwide, and today the movement is underway throughout the UK, as well as in many parts of Europe, Asia, North America, Australia, Africa and the Caribbean. Keswick Ministries is committed to strengthen the network in the UK and beyond, through prayer, news, pioneering and cooperative activity.

- **Keswick resources**. Keswick Ministries is producing a growing range of books and booklets based on the core foundations of Christian life and mission. It makes Bible teaching available through free access to mp3 downloads, and the sale of DVDs and CDs. It broadcasts online through Clayton TV and annual BBC Radio 4 services. In addition to the summer Convention, Keswick Ministries is hoping to develop other teaching and training events in the coming years.

Our unity

The Keswick movement worldwide has adopted a key Pauline statement to describe its gospel inclusivity: 'for you are all one in Christ Jesus' (Galatians 3:28). Keswick Ministries works with evangelicals from a wide variety of church backgrounds, on the understanding that they share a commitment to the essential truths of the Christian faith as set out in our statement of belief.

Our contact details

Mail: Keswick Ministries, Keswick Convention Centre,
Skiddaw Street, Keswick, CA12 4BY England
T: 017687 80075
E: info@keswickministries.org
W: www.keswickministries.org

Related titles from IVP

KESWICK FOUNDATIONS

Mission Matters
Love Says Go
Tim Chester

ISBN: 978–1–78359–280–7
176 pages, paperback

The Father delights in his Son. This is the starting point of mission, its very core. The word 'mission' means 'sending'. But for many centuries this was only used to describe what God did, sending his Son and his Spirit into the world. World mission exists because the Father wants people to delight in his Son, and the Son wants people to delight in the Father.

In this companion volume to *Sent: Serving God's Mission*, Tim Chester introduces us to a cascade of love: love flowing from the Father to the Son through the Spirit. And that love overflows and, through us, keeps on flowing to our Christian community and beyond, to a needy world. Mission matters. This book is for ordinary individuals willing to step out and be part of the most amazing, exciting venture in the history of the world.

Praise:

'If you want to fire up your church with a vision for global mission, this is your book! . . . It should carry a spiritual health warning.' **David Coffey OBE**

'I am sure this book will provoke many to respond to the challenge as they realize that there are still thousands waiting to be introduced to the Saviour.' **Helen Roseveare**

Related titles from IVP

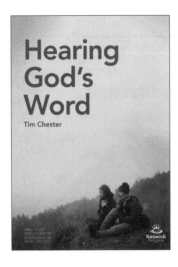

KESWICK STUDY GUIDE

Hearing God's Word
Tim Chester

ISBN: 978–1–78359–581–5

80 pages, paperback

What has God said? How has he said it? And how does it apply to our lives today?

Hearing God's Word invites us to explore these questions and more.

Each session starts with an introduction to the topic and then moves to a Bible passage. We focus on the theme, go deeper and explore living out the word in our daily life. Useful prayer prompts also help to make the message real and personal.

Praise:

'Biblical, practical, devotional and thoughtful. An excellent resource for group or personal study to strengthen our convictions about the truth of the Bible, and enable us to discover its riches for ourselves.' **John Risbridger**

'Here is a workable, practical guide that will help you to study the Bible by yourself or with others. Used well, it will help you grow in your faith.' **Ian Coffey**

Related titles from IVP

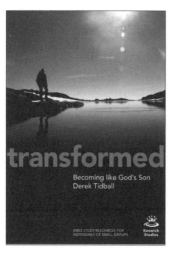

KESWICK STUDY GUIDE

Transformed
Becoming Like God's Son
Derek Tidball

ISBN: 978–1–78359–454–2
80 pages, paperback

Becoming like Jesus requires us not just to meet him occasionally but also steadily and surely to 'remain' in him.

How does this look close up?

In a world where Christlikeness is counter-cultural, the author offers sure-footed Bible teaching, questions, illustrations, suggestions and prayers to point us in the right direction. And, as well as this useful material, we have the Holy Spirit's help to live transformed lives today.

This practical, thought-provoking and accessible resource is another addition to the popular IVP/Keswick Ministries series of study guides.

Praise:

'Yes, the terrain is challenging. But this is a grace-filled, Christ-dependent journey to become more like Jesus. Come join!' **Tracy Cotterell**

Available from your local Christian bookshop or **www.ivpbooks.com**